Original title:
Embracing Emotional Ebb and Flow

Copyright © 2024 Swan Charm
All rights reserved.

Author: Johan Kirsipuu
ISBN HARDBACK: 978-9916-86-575-0
ISBN PAPERBACK: 978-9916-86-576-7
ISBN EBOOK: 978-9916-86-577-4

The Unseen Currents We Navigate

In the silence, whispers sway,
Guiding us through night and day.
Unseen forces, pull and guide,
In our hearts, they do abide.

Through the shadows, pathways weave,
Every choice, we must believe.
Moments drift like leaves in air,
Finding meaning everywhere.

Raindrops on a Wanting Soul

Raindrops kiss the thirsty ground,
Echoes of a yearning sound.
Softly falling, dreams take flight,
Hopes reborn in muted light.

Each drop tells a tale untold,
Of love's warmth and passion bold.
Through the storm, we find our way,
In the puddles, shadows play.

Serendipity in Shifting Tides

Waves roll in, a dance of fate,
Life unfolds, we navigate.
With every tide, new paths arise,
In the chaos, beauty lies.

Fortune smiles on hearts that roam,
Finding joy in every home.
Connections form, like stars align,
In the vastness, all is fine.

The Depths Beneath the Waves

Beneath the surface, secrets flow,
In the depths, where few will go.
Mysteries hidden, dark and deep,
Whispered tales, the ocean keeps.

Creatures dwell in shadows cast,
Echoes of the ocean's past.
In the silence, truths reside,
A world where dreams and fears collide.

The Calm Before the Waves

The ocean lies still, a glassy sheet,
Whispers of peace in the air so sweet.
Clouds drift lazily, shadows in play,
Nature holds breath, awaiting the fray.

The horizon glows, a soft peach hue,
A promise of chaos, with tides breaking through.
Birds dance above in the warm evening light,
Unaware of the storms that approach in the night.

Chasing the Sun After the Rain

Puddles reflect the sky's bright embrace,
Children jump high, splashes fill the space.
Rainbows emerge, colors vivid and bold,
Nature's true treasure, a sight to behold.

Footsteps on paths where water once pooled,
Chasing the sun, where light has been ruled.
Laughter rings out, a joyful refrain,
Hearts lifted high, free from the pain.

Balancing Between the Storm

Clouds rumble low, a warning to heed,
Trees sway and bend, to the will of the breeze.
Lightning strikes, a dance made in fright,
Stars hidden away, lost in the night.

Yet in the tempest, a calm can be found,
Moments of stillness, where peace wraps around.
In the chaos, a flicker of grace,
Holding on tight, to this fragile space.

Bridges Built on Shifting Sands

Footprints fade slowly, as tides come and go,
Wonders of time in the ebb and the flow.
Bridges to nowhere, yet sturdy and grand,
Mapping the journeys through vast, barren land.

Waves crash and whisper, secrets they keep,
Navigating dreams while the world's fast asleep.
Sand meets the sky, a canvas untamed,
The heart learns to flourish, despite being shamed.

Clusters of Clouds and Celestial Hues

In the sky, soft whispers play,
Colors dance at close of day.
Brush of pink and strokes of grey,
Nature's palette, bright and gay.

Clouds drift like thoughts in the air,
Fleeting dreams that wander where.
Weaving tales with gentle care,
Sketching stories, light and rare.

Sunset paints with golden grace,
Fluffy clusters start to chase.
Shadows stretch and softly trace,
Moments lost in time and space.

Night unveils its velvet shroud,
Stars emerge from silence loud.
In the dark, these treasures crowd,
Nature whispers, pure and proud.

Beneath the vast celestial sphere,
We find peace, we hold it near.
In the clusters, hearts will steer,
Chasing dreams, our souls sincere.

Heartbeats in the Sea of Change

Waves crash upon the sandy shore,
Echoes of a tale, evermore.
Time slips through like grains of sand,
In this dance, we understand.

With each pulse, the ocean sighs,
Reflecting tides, as daylight dies.
In the depths, our memories dwell,
Rhythms formed, we know them well.

Seasons shift with gentle grace,
In this sea, we find our place.
Moments rise, then fade away,
Yet heartbeats linger, night and day.

Change a melody, sweet and fine,
Every crest and trough, a line.
In the current, we refine,
The art of living, hearts entwined.

Through the storms, we learn to breathe,
In the ebb, our hopes retrieve.
With every heartbeat, we believe,
In the sea's embrace, we weave.

Lanterns in the Fog

In the mist, soft glimmers glow,
Lanterns swaying to and fro.
Guiding hearts through paths unknown,
In the fog, we are not alone.

Every beam a whisper sweet,
Flickering hope beneath our feet.
Through the haze, a way appears,
Washing doubts, calming fears.

As the night wraps tight around,
In each lantern, love is found.
To the lost, they shine so bright,
Leading souls to find the light.

Fog may shroud the stars above,
Yet these lanterns speak of love.
Through the shadows, we will roam,
Finding solace, finding home.

With each step, a warm embrace,
In the dark, we find our place.
Lanterns guide in puzzling night,
Kindling hearts, igniting sight.

Churning Seas of the Inner Landscape

Waves of thought begin to swell,
In this mind, a secret well.
Tides of feelings, deep and wide,
Churning seas where dreams abide.

Currents pull, they twist and turn,
Lessons hidden, fires burn.
In the depths, the silence speaks,
Whispers soft, through valleys bleak.

Storm clouds gather, shadows cast,
In this journey, find the past.
Churning waters, fierce and bold,
Every ripple, a truth told.

Through the chaos, we emerge,
Finding strength in every surge.
With each wave, we learn to stand,
Navigating through this land.

In the stillness, peace can bloom,
From the depths, we chase the gloom.
Churning seas will guide our way,
In the landscape, life holds sway.

Navigating Through the Depths

In shadows deep, where few have tread,
A whisper calls, where dreams are bred.
Through murky waves, we lose our way,
Yet stars above still guide the fray.

With every stroke, a whispering sea,
Unfolds the secrets, sets us free.
In currents strong, our souls will dance,
Embracing fear, we take the chance.

The depths conceal what we must find,
A melody of heart and mind.
We brave the storms that wreck the night,
For in the dark, we seek the light.

Our vessel worn, but spirits high,
We navigate beneath the sky.
In silence deep, a truth unveils,
A tale of journeys, lost in gales.

So let the ocean's call ring true,
In depths unknown, we'll find what's new.
With every wave, a lesson shared,
In navigating life, we dare.

Petals Floating on a Breeze

Softly drifting, petals fall,
Whispers of spring, a gentle call.
Carried away on a tender sigh,
In fleeting moments, time slips by.

Colors dance upon the air,
Nature's brush, beyond compare.
Each petal tells a tale once spun,
In the warmth of the golden sun.

Floating lightly, with grace they roam,
Finding solace, far from home.
In the breeze, their joy released,
In quietude, their hearts find peace.

As seasons change and memories fade,
Each petal's journey, a blissful cascade.
Though they drift, their beauty stays,
In hearts they touch, throughout our days.

With every gust, a story flows,
Of love and loss, the heart well knows.
So let them soar, on high they tease,
In life's embrace, like petals, we breeze.

The Tide That Binds Us

In rhythmic waves, our hearts align,
The ocean's pulse, a sacred sign.
With every ebb, we feel the pull,
A bond that whispers, deep and full.

Together we rise, together we fall,
In tides that mark our journey's call.
Through storms that shake the shores we know,
Our spirits weave, like ebb and flow.

The moon above casts silver light,
Illuminating paths in night.
As waters dance and foam does churn,
In every tide, our souls will learn.

Though distance separates our shore,
The tide will bring you back once more.
In currents strong, our hearts entwined,
Through every wave, our love defined.

So let the ocean's song resound,
In every heartbeat, love is found.
Through every tide, we will remain,
Forever bound, despite the rain.

A Symphony of Laughter and Sorrow

In shadowed halls where echoes play,
Laughter twines with sorrow's sway.
Each note a jewel, both bright and gray,
In music's weave, we find our way.

The high notes spring like joyous light,
While lows descend into the night.
Together they create the song,
A melody where we belong.

With every breath, a tale unfolds,
Of dreams pursued and hearts consoled.
In harmony, both pain and bliss,
We dance within such sweet abyss.

So let us sing through tears and cheer,
In symphonies, our truths are clear.
For every heart that breaks and mends,
The music carries, never ends.

In laughter shared, in sorrow's plea,
We find the strength to simply be.
A symphony of life and grace,
In every note, we find our place.

Beneath the Glimmer of a Silvered Sky

Stars wink softly in the night,
Whispers of dreams take their flight.
Clouds drift gently, lace on air,
Beneath the glimmer, hearts lay bare.

Moonlight dances on the ground,
In silent tales, the lost are found.
Moments linger, softly sigh,
Beneath the glimmer of a silvered sky.

Hope ignites the darkened space,
In every shadow, find a trace.
Fleeting warm breaths, long and slow,
Beneath the glimmer, light will grow.

Gentle breezes weave through trees,
Embracing whispers, soothing pleas.
Nature's song, a lullaby,
Beneath the glimmer, dreams won't die.

In quiet corners, visions bloom,
Casting light dispels the gloom.
The universe, vast and high,
Beneath the glimmer, souls can fly.

The Poems of Highs and Lows

In echoes deep, the silence speaks,
Of fleeting days and winding peaks.
A journey carved through joy and pain,
The poems of highs and lows remain.

With every rise, there comes a fall,
The heart's soft rhythm, a constant call.
In valleys low, in mountains high,
The poems of life convince us why.

Moments shimmer, like stars at night,
Guiding us through shadow and light.
In the dance of fate, we learn to cry,
The poems of highs and lows draw nigh.

Hope ignites on the steady climb,
Grief mellows with the passing time.
Each line written, a gentle sigh,
The poems of highs and lows imply.

Through tears and laughter, we will roam,
Crafting verses, finding home.
In every heartbeat, dreams comply,
The poems of highs and lows will fly.

Charms of Calm and Turbulence

Waves crash softly on sandy shores,
In the dance of peace, uncertainty roars.
A gentle breeze whispers a name,
Charms of calm and turbulence, both the same.

Time stands still in the eye of the storm,
Yet in disarray, we find the norm.
Hearts beat wildly, yet spirits retain,
Charms of calm and turbulence in refrain.

Through chaos and quiet, we find our place,
In fleeting moments, a warm embrace.
Like twilight merging with the day,
Charms of calm and turbulent sway.

Life's rhythm flows like ebbing tides,
In every doubt, a strength resides.
In peace and struggle, we learn to play,
Charms of calm and turbulence lead the way.

With every heartbeat, a choice unfolds,
In silence and storm, life bolds.
Through every tear, through every ray,
Charms of calm and turbulence will stay.

Emotions like Ocean Spray

Whispers echo in the salty air,
Feelings rise like waves, laid bare.
Joy and sorrow, vast and free,
Emotions like ocean spray, flow endlessly.

Tides of laughter, waves of pain,
In heartbeat rhythms, love remains.
Each splash paints a memory, bright and gray,
Emotions like ocean spray, come what may.

The horizon stretches, dreams collide,
In every ebb, there's a burgeoning tide.
Through storms and sunlight, find your way,
Emotions like ocean spray, drifting sway.

Seagulls soar on winds of fate,
Guiding souls to navigate.
In every journey, life's ballet,
Emotions like ocean spray, always play.

With the moon's pull, hearts align,
In every droplet, a glimpse divine.
In this vast sea, we'll find our stay,
Emotions like ocean spray, here to stay.

Melodies of the Mind's Ocean

In the depths where thoughts reside,
Waves of whispers start to glide.
Echoes linger, soft and free,
Creating tunes of memory.

Dreams like currents ebb and flow,
Guiding where the heart might go.
Harmony in tides that swell,
Crafting stories we can't tell.

Ripples dance upon the shore,
Each one holds a tale of yore.
Melodies that gently blend,
Finding peace as feelings mend.

The vast expanse, a canvas wide,
Colors blend as visions collide.
In this ocean, we explore,
The melodies we can't ignore.

As the skies begin to part,
Songs of solace fill the heart.
In the sea of thought we find,
The gentle rhythms of the mind.

Serenity in the Storm

Amidst the thunder's fierce embrace,
Quiet moments find their place.
Lightning flashes, bright and bold,
Yet tranquil hearts refuse to fold.

In the chaos, calm can rise,
Like a whisper in the skies.
Raindrops sing a lullaby,
Softening the tempest's cry.

Winds may howl, but here we stand,
Finding stillness, hand in hand.
Nature's fury, fierce and grand,
Teaches peace in every strand.

Through the swirl and through the fray,
Inner light will guide the way.
Even storms will pass and fade,
Leaving clarity well laid.

Serenity blooms in the strife,
Reminding us of nature's life.
In the storm, we clearly see,
Beauty hides in chaos free.

Embracing the Shifting Sands

Footprints fade with every breeze,
Changes flow with graceful ease.
Each grain tells a tale profound,
Of journeys lost and wisdom found.

Desert winds sing soft and low,
Carving shapes where memories flow.
In the dunes, the heart can roam,
Within the shifting sands, we're home.

Time will dance on golden tides,
As the vast horizon strides.
Embrace the ebb and flow of light,
In the darkness, find your sight.

Every step a lesson learned,
Every twist, a dream discerned.
Through the ages, tides will shift,
Through the sand, the soul will lift.

So let us wander, let us chase,
The shifting sands that time will grace.
In their embrace, we will find,
A deeper truth within the mind.

The Rhythm of Inner Waters

Beneath the surface, currents pulse,
In stillness, magic starts to convulse.
Waves of thought, soft and bright,
Flow together, finding light.

Rivers run through valleys deep,
Whispers echoed, dreams we keep.
In the flow, the heart reveals,
Mysteries that time conceals.

Before the dawn, a silent song,
Every heartbeat, we belong.
Gentle ripples, strong yet clear,
Guide us on through doubt and fear.

In the depths, where shadows play,
Flows the rhythm of the day.
Navigating unseen streams,
Carving paths through silent dreams.

Let us dive into the flow,
Where the inner waters glow.
In the rhythm, find your peace,
Let the waters never cease.

Desert Blooms from Rain's Return

In a land where silence reigns,
Soft whispers of hope remain.
The skies weep gentle tears,
Bringing life through all the years.

Cacti bloom with colors bright,
Underneath the silver light.
Petals dance in warm embrace,
Nature's gift, a sweet solace.

From parched earth, new dreams arise,
In the air, the fragrance lies.
Every droplet, pure and clear,
Stirs the heart, dispels the fear.

Sunlit rays on blossoms play,
A glimpse of life in bright array.
From barren lands to lush terrain,
The desert sings of rain's refrain.

As the storm clouds start to part,
Hope takes root deep in the heart.
Desert blooms, a sight to see,
A testament to vitality.

Riding the Rollercoaster of Being

Life twists and turns, a thrilling ride,
With moments of joy that coincide.
Laughter flies on the winds of change,
While sorrow and joy are interchanged.

Up we soar to the heights of glee,
Then plunge down low, a stormy sea.
Each loop and turn teaches us more,
To embrace the chaos and adore.

Ever shifting, the track does weave,
Lessons hidden, if we believe.
To hold on tight through every strife,
Is the essence, the thrill of life.

In the rush, we find our peace,
Through every dip, our souls release.
Riding high on a wave of dreams,
Life's tapestry is never what it seems.

So let's embrace each drop and climb,
For in this ride, we dance with time.
With hearts wide open, we shall see,
The art of living, wild and free.

The Balance of Sun and Shadows

Morning light spills soft and gold,
Painting stories yet untold.
Shadows stretch and dance about,
In a world where dreams sprout.

Golden warmth and cool embrace,
Together, they find their place.
In the twilight, colors blend,
Where beginnings meet the end.

Each moment holds a secret key,
Unlocking what we're meant to be.
As sun retreats, the stars ignite,
Guiding us through the velvet night.

In the whispers of the breeze,
Lies a balance, meant to please.
Both joy and sorrow intertwine,
Life's great dance, a grand design.

So let the sun and shadows play,
In harmony, they find their way.
Embrace the light, give darkness grace,
Together, they create time's space.

Castles Built on Shifting Sands

In the desert, dreams take shape,
Constructed high, no room for fate.
Towers rise towards the sky,
Yet crumble down with each swift sigh.

The winds whisper tales of yore,
Of castles built on hope's own floor.
Fragile dreams in shifting light,
Erode beneath the starry night.

Every grain tells a story grand,
Of hearts that dared to make a stand.
With every wave, foundations sway,
Yet still we build, come what may.

So let us craft from sands of time,
A monument for hearts that climb.
In impermanence, we find our might,
For every fall brings forth new height.

With every gust, we take the chance,
To redefine the precious dance.
Castles rise, then fade away,
But dreams will live, come what may.

Flowing with the River of Feelings

Feelings flow like a river wide,
Carrying whispers of heart's true tide.
Gentle ripples in the soft light,
Shadows dancing in the night.

Beneath the surface, secrets lie,
Currents swift, they weave and sigh.
Emotions shift like the swift breeze,
Bringing solace, bringing unease.

Water sings a familiar tune,
Underneath the glowing moon.
With every wave, a story starts,
A journey deep within our hearts.

Edging closer to the shore,
Memories linger, longing for more.
Capturing moments as they drift by,
In the river's embrace, we learn to fly.

Flowing onward, always free,
Where hopes and fears entwine, you see.
Each twist and turn reveals the grace,
Of life's river, our sacred space.

Nature's Palette of Sad and Glad

In forests deep where shadows play,
Nature speaks in hues of gray.
A sorrowful breeze whispers low,
Among the branches, tales of woe.

Yet golden rays can pierce the gloom,
Morning dew awakens bloom.
With every drop, a joy is found,
As laughter dances all around.

A symphony of color bright,
Painted sunsets kiss the night.
In petals soft, both joy and pain,
Life's dual essence we entertain.

Mountains stand, both strong and tall,
In their shadows, we rise and fall.
With every storm, a cleansing rain,
Nature's canvas feels our strain.

So embrace the shades, both dark and light,
In every heart, a spark ignites.
Nature's palette tells our tale,
Of sadness found, and joy set sail.

Beneath the Storm Clouds' Veil

Beneath the storm clouds, shadows grow,
Whispers of thunder begin to flow.
Lightning flashes, a bright surprise,
In the darkness, beauty lies.

Raindrops tap on the windowpane,
Nature's tears, a sweet refrain.
Each droplet holds a story's weight,
Of trials faced and love's small fate.

The winds howl like a wild beast,
Riding the chaos, fears released.
Yet after cries, the calm arrives,
In storm's embrace, the spirit thrives.

Colors bright emerge anew,
After the rain, a clearer view.
Life's echo in the sky above,
A dance of pain, a dance of love.

So let the tempests come and go,
For in their wake, our hearts will grow.
Choosing courage, we prevail,
Beneath the storm clouds' sacred veil.

Unraveling Layers of Heartstrings

In silence deep, heartstrings play,
Melodies only love can sway.
Threads of joy entwined with fear,
In each note, a whispered tear.

Unraveling tales of yesterdays,
Where memories linger, sweet warm rays.
Each layer peeled reveals the truth,
Of fragile hope and fleeting youth.

A tapestry of laughter, pain,
Crafted through sunshine and rain.
Woven tightly, yet they fray,
As time moves on, they fade away.

With every strum, a beating heart,
In this dance, we play our part.
Finding harmony in the strife,
The strings remind us, this is life.

So let them sing, these tender threads,
Embrace the love, the tears we've shed.
For in the music, we are free,
Unraveling layers, just you and me.

Driftwood Dreams and Ocean Echoes

In twilight's sigh, the driftwood rests,
Whispers of waves in ancient quests.
Salt-kissed air, a lover's breath,
Holding stories of life and death.

Carved by time, the wood reveals,
Silent truths that water steals.
Echoes dance on the shoreline's edge,
Reminders that we too must pledge.

Beneath the stars, the sea unfolds,
A tapestry of dreams retold.
Each ripple sings of distant lands,
Imprinted softly in shifting sands.

Among the shells, old secrets lie,
Not all the dreams are born to fly.
Yet in the night, they drift and sway,
Carried gently, like hopes that play.

In every tide, a promise flows,
Of tomorrow's light where journey goes.
From driftwood dreams, we too arise,
To chase the dawn beyond the skies.

Symphony of the Sinking and Surfacing

In ocean's depths, silence swells,
A symphony of haunting bells.
Drowning notes in water's grasp,
Breathless sighs that fade and clasp.

From shadows deep, a tune emerges,
Sonorous waves, the soul purges.
Each rising swell, a story told,
From crashing surf to whispers bold.

In twilight hues, the seabirds dive,
A dance that keeps the dream alive.
With every crash, the heartbeats quick,
The pulse of life, a rhythm thick.

As tides retreat, the echoes fade,
Yet memories linger, softly laid.
In every wave, a cry for more,
A symphony along the shore.

In every die and every rise,
The ocean hums its lullabies.
A haunting blend of dark and light,
In sinking sands, we take to flight.

A Journal of Dune and Wave

Footprints etched in shifting grains,
Tales told by the frothy stains.
A journal written in sun and foam,
Where each wave finds a way back home.

Beneath the sun, the dunes do sigh,
As wisps of wind drift softly by.
A canvas where the tides compose,
Stories hidden, only nature knows.

Seashells speak in colors bright,
Carrying tales of day and night.
In every shell, a whispered truth,
Of aged adventures, lost in youth.

Through the cerulean lens we see,
The ebb and flow of destiny.
Each rising wave, a turn of page,
In this ocean book, we write with sage.

With every sunset, stories blend,
A timeless journey without end.
The dunes will shift, and waves will flow,
In tales of life, forever grow.

The Spectrum of Feelings Unfurled

In azure depth, emotions swirl,
A wide expanse, the heart's own pearl.
From joy to sorrow, shades abound,
In ocean's heart, our souls are found.

The crashing waves, they shout and sing,
An anthem born of everything.
With every crest, a vision pressed,
In harmony, we find our quest.

Calm waters hold a gentle grace,
Reflecting dreams in tender space.
Yet tempests rise, like fears unchained,
In raging storms, our hope is strained.

But through the winds, we learn to steer,
Embracing both the crisp and sheer.
For in the tide's embrace we learn,
The spectrum calls, and hearts return.

In every wave, a feeling glows,
The colors blend as love bestows.
For each emotion, vast and wide,
Is but a journey, tide by tide.

The Palette of Joy and Grief

In colors bright, the heart does dance,
Through hues of laughter, love's romance.
Yet shadows creep, in deeper tones,
In sorrow's grip, our spirit moans.

Brush strokes of time, we blend and paint,
With whispered dreams, and moments faint.
The canvas holds both light and woe,
A masterpiece of ebb and flow.

In vibrant reds, our passions flare,
While blues, like teardrops, fill the air.
Each shade a story, rich and deep,
In joy and grief, our souls we keep.

Where yellow shines, the sun breaks through,
In purple whispers, night bids adieu.
We paint our lives with every sigh,
In every stroke, we laugh and cry.

So let the palette softly blend,
A testament, when colors mend.
For in this art, our truths unfold,
In joy and grief, our hearts consoled.

Ripples of Unspoken Truth

In still waters, secrets lie,
Beneath the surface, whispers sigh.
Ripples form with each unheard plea,
An echo calls, yet none can see.

The weight of words we leave unsaid,
Haunts the heart, where silence treads.
Like stones dropped in a quiet lake,
The waves of thought, they gently shake.

Yet courage blooms in timid hearts,
To speak the truth that tearing starts.
In fragile tones, we find our voice,
And in the night, we make our choice.

Each ripple spreads, a tale unfolds,
In hidden depths, our fate beholds.
The honest heart, though scared and shy,
Creates a sound too pure to die.

So let the ripples dance and play,
Illuminate what hides away.
For in the truth, we learn to trust,
In every drop, igniting gust.

A Journey Through the Mist

The morning fog, a cloak of dreams,
It veils the world in silent themes.
With every step, the path unclear,
Yet hope and wonder draw us near.

Through shrouded roads where shadows dwell,
Our hearts beat softly, a fleeting spell.
In whispered winds, the secrets flow,
Each twist and turn, a tale to know.

The mist conceals, yet hints of light,
A glimmer shines, breaking the night.
With every foggy bend we take,
A chance to rise, to bend, to break.

In silent woods where echoes roam,
We find our way, we make it home.
Through swirling thoughts, both light and dim,
The journey calls, we dive in thin.

So let the mist embrace our quest,
For in the haze, we find our rest.
A journey woven, both lost and found,
In every step, magic unbound.

Soft Serenades of Solitude

Beneath the stars, the quiet breathes,
In solitude, the spirit weaves.
A lullaby in shadows cast,
Where whispered dreams are held steadfast.

The gentle night, a warming light,
In soft embrace, we find our flight.
Through hallowed spaces, calm and deep,
In solitude, our secrets keep.

Each note that lingers, sweet and slow,
Unveils the heart's most tender glow.
The serenade of silent thought,
In precious moments, love is wrought.

So let the stillness wrap around,
In solitude, our souls are found.
Each fleeting sigh, a song to share,
In soft serenades, we lay bare.

In quietude, our hearts take flight,
Embracing peace, a pure delight.
For in the music of the night,
We find our truth, our guiding light.

Waves of Inner Whisper

Waves crash softly on the shore,
Whispers of the deep, evermore.
Secrets held in ocean's sigh,
Echoes of dreams that drift and fly.

Moonlit nights bring calm and peace,
Carrying thoughts, a sweet release.
Every crest holds tales untold,
In the silence, hearts unfold.

Beneath the surface, currents sway,
Guiding souls along the way.
In the depths, we find our fate,
As the tide decides our state.

Winds of change will gently steer,
Through the tempests, we persevere.
With every swell, we learn to trust,
In the water, we find our must.

Together, we ride the infinite sea,
Finding solace, just you and me.
Waves of wisdom, vast and grand,
In every whisper, a guiding hand.

Tides of Heartfelt Reflection

Tides roll in with tender grace,
Washing worries from our face.
In the ebb, we search for light,
In the flow, we find what's right.

Moments lost in deep embrace,
Time suspended, a sacred space.
With every wave, our hearts align,
Drawing strength from love's design.

Memories dance within the foam,
Each ripple calls us softly home.
Healing whispers, sweet and low,
Tide of stories, soft and slow.

As the ocean meets the sky,
So too do our dreams comply.
In the stillness of the night,
Hearts awaken, taking flight.

Together we stand, hand in hand,
Guided by waves upon the sand.
In the rhythm, we find our way,
Tides of love, here to stay.

The Dance of Rising Tears

Teardrops fall like rain, they say,
Each one brings a brand new day.
In the dance of joy and pain,
We discover loss, we gain.

Spirals of sorrow, gently twirl,
Memories within them swirl.
In the depths, our spirits weave,
Beauty found in what we grieve.

With every tear, a story grows,
Unraveling what the heart knows.
Carried forth by winds of change,
In the hurt, we find what's strange.

Yet through the ache, there's brightness too,
In every shadow, a glimmering hue.
For in the tears, we come alive,
Learning more of how to thrive.

So let them flow, these gifts of grace,
As emotions take their rightful place.
In the dance of rising tears,
We find the courage to face our fears.

When Shadows Kiss the Light

Softly whispers in the night,
When shadows kiss the gentle light.
In between the dark and bright,
We find peace, our hearts' delight.

Flickers of hope against the gloom,
A promise shared, a flower's bloom.
In this dance of dusk and dawn,
We rise anew, forever drawn.

Moments pause under silver skies,
Truth unveiled through longing sighs.
As daylight fades, the stars appear,
Guiding us through what we fear.

Together, we embrace the night,
When shadows blend and hearts take flight.
In the twilight's warm embrace,
We find solace, a sacred space.

So let the shadows lead the way,
For in the dark, there's light to play.
When shadows kiss the light so bright,
We weave our dreams, taking flight.

Beneath the Surface: Reaching Deep

In shadows cast by silent waves,
A world awaits, where silence craves.
Whispers dance through currents blue,
Hidden tales of those who knew.

Ancient secrets, softly told,
In depths where time is slow and bold.
The pulse of life beneath the skin,
A journey starts, the dive begins.

With every breath, the heart does race,
In liquid realms, we find our place.
Beneath the surface, dreams take flight,
As shadows merge with fading light.

A symphony of creatures play,
In darkened depths, they find their way.
With gentle grace, they weave their art,
A canvas painted with every heart.

Emerging now, the sun's embrace,
Reflections shimmer, a warm trace.
We surface with new stories to keep,
Beneath the surface, we reached deep.

Sailing Through Stormy Skies

Winds howl fierce, the ship does sway,
Beneath the clouds, both dark and gray.
With sails unfurled, we brave the night,
Through tempest's roar, we seek the light.

Each wave a mountain, crashing high,
Yet hearts are strong, we will not die.
Together we push through the strain,
As thunder drums a wild refrain.

Stars are lost, with hope unseen,
But faith remains, a steady dream.
Through stormy skies, our spirits soar,
As we navigate to distant shore.

In every gust, we find our song,
With courage deep, we will be strong.
To sail through storms, a test of will,
A journey forged, a heart to fill.

And when the skies at last turn blue,
The calm returns, the thrill anew.
With every wave, a tale to weave,
In sailing through, we learn to believe.

Reflections on a Glassy Sea

A mirror deep, the ocean sleeps,
Where sunlight dances, silence creeps.
Reflections shimmer, secrets hide,
In tranquil depths, where dreams abide.

Each ripple holds a fleeting thought,
A moment caught, a lesson taught.
With every glance, the past awakes,
In pools of calm, the heart remakes.

Beneath the surface, stories flow,
A quiet place where whispers grow.
The glassy sea, a canvas wide,
In stillness calm, our souls reside.

From shores we stand and gaze in awe,
At every hue, each shift we draw.
It's in the peace we find our way,
Reflections linger, bright and gray.

With every wave, the world does change,
Yet in this space, we're never strange.
A glassy sea, a gentle seam,
In still reflection, we dare to dream.

Tidal Thoughts and Tempestuous Dreams

The tide rolls in, a whispered thought,
Each wave a wish, a battle fought.
In salty air, we breathe the night,
With tempest dreams that spark the light.

Shores will shift, yet hearts remain,
In every rise, the pulse of pain.
But with each fall, we find our way,
In tidal thoughts, the night turns day.

A restless mind, like ocean's roar,
In storms of doubt, we seek for more.
Through swirling winds, our hopes ascend,
In realms where dreams and tides can blend.

The moon above, a guiding hand,
As we navigate through sea and sand.
With every ebb, a chance to grow,
In tidal thoughts, the spirit flows.

Together, we embrace the sway,
With open hands, we trust the play.
In tempest's grasp, our dreams ignite,
In tidal thoughts, we rise to fight.

Footprints in the Sand of Time

Footprints fade on the shore,
Whispers of tales long gone.
Each mark a fleeting dream,
Vanishing before the dawn.

The tide pulls them away,
Yet memories remain bright.
The past, a gentle echo,
Guiding through the night.

With every step we take,
We carve our stories deep.
Time's embrace is soft,
In its arms, we will keep.

Moments slip like sand,
Through fingers not so sure.
Our journey, sweet and vast,
In the heart, it endures.

Each footprint left behind,
Is a mark of who we are.
In the sands of time,
We shine like a distant star.

Tidal Changes of the Heart

Waves crash against the shore,
Mending hearts that bleed.
In the rhythm of the sea,
We find the strength we need.

The tide pulls love away,
But brings it back once more.
An ebb and flow of feeling,
An open, aching door.

With every tide that comes,
New hopes begin to form.
In the depths of longing,
We weather every storm.

Rising with the moonlight,
Our hearts reach for the sky.
In this dance of longing,
We'll learn how to fly.

Amidst the waves of change,
We'll find a steady beat.
In the ocean of our souls,
Love's currents feel so sweet.

Journey through Storms and Stillness

Underneath the darkened skies,
Thunder rumbles near.
Yet in the stillness following,
Calm will reappear.

We sail through raging tempests,
The wind a fierce embrace.
With courage as our beacon,
We'll find our way, our place.

The storm may steal our breath,
Yet the calm will restore.
In the pause between the waves,
We learn to love once more.

Each challenge faced with valor,
Winds that shape our souls,
Transforming fear to power,
In the heart, we become whole.

Through seasons of uncertainty,
We'll gather strength anew.
In the midst of every storm,
Our dreams guide us through.

A Heart's Compass Amidst the Waves

In the ocean's vast embrace,
A compass points us true.
With every wave that crashes,
We discover what is due.

The stars above are shining,
Guiding paths unknown.
With courage in our hearts,
We'll find our way back home.

Each gust that sweeps around,
Is a whisper from the past.
In the dance of tides and winds,
We learn to hold on fast.

A heart's compass will lead us,
Through the tumult and strife.
For in the flow of waters,
We navigate our life.

In this journey through the waves,
We'll rise against the storm.
With a heart that knows the way,
We always will transform.

Reflections of Sunlight on Water

The sun dips low, a painted sky,
Ripples dance where the waters lie.
Golden hues on azure waves,
Nature whispers, and the heart saves.

Each shimmer tells a tale untold,
Mirrored dreams in liquid gold.
A fleeting spark, a moment's grace,
Life reflected in this embrace.

Soft breezes lend a tender touch,
The water listens, it knows so much.
In quiet depths, secrets remain,
In every drop, joy and pain.

As evening falls, the colors blend,
A tranquil space where shadows bend.
Fractured light on gentle shores,
In stillness, the heart restores.

The dance of sun on water's face,
A timeless, pure, and sacred place.
Each moment glimmers, yet is gone,
In twilight's glow, forever drawn.

Harmony in Dissonance

In frayed notes, beauty unfolds,
A cacophony, a rhythm bold.
Voices clash yet intertwine,
In discord, a melody divine.

Rough edges that beautifully collide,
In every clash, emotions ride.
Chaos sings with vibrant flair,
In the silence, a breath of air.

Like shattered glass, refracted light,
Each fracture sparkles, ignites the night.
The outcast calls, we hear its plea,
In dissonance, we find our key.

Threads of chaos, woven tight,
Together create a tapestry bright.
In every note, a story's thread,
Harmony blooms where fears have fled.

With open hearts, let music sway,
In wild rhythms, find our way.
Embrace the clash, the sweet dismay,
For in the noise, we learn to play.

The Tide Pools of Memory

Cradled by rocks, a world preserved,
In pools of time, the heart observed.
Waves of the past gently recede,
Whispers of nostalgia, buried seed.

A starfish clings to slippery stone,
Past echoes of joy, of feeling alone.
Each ripple stirs a buried thought,
In quiet moments, wisdom sought.

Shells hold secrets of distant seas,
Each one sings a memory's breeze.
The tide rolls in, the tide rolls out,
In vastness, we find what it's about.

Colors of life in salt and sun,
In every pool, a journey begun.
Moments captured in salty air,
In fragile beauty, our souls laid bare.

When storms might crash and darkness fall,
The tide pools stand, steadfast and tall.
In every glance, a world unfolds,
In memories, our heart's truth holds.

Emotions, a River of Colors

A river flows with colors bright,
Emotion's depth, both dark and light.
Crimson joy and sapphire peace,
The currents speak and never cease.

In gentle waves, soft whispers glide,
Violet shadows, where feelings hide.
Beneath the surface, storms may brew,
In every ripple, a story true.

Golden laughter dances free,
Emerald hopes, wild and carefree.
Each hue a pulse, a breath of fate,
In every shade, we resonate.

The river bends, a path unknown,
In every twist, our heart has grown.
From quiet depths to raging flow,
In colors bright, our spirits glow.

A palette formed from joy and strife,
In every brush, we paint our life.
With every stroke, emotions blend,
In this river, our souls transcend.

The Path of Ever-Changing Currents

Through winding rivers bright and wide,
The currents pull, the waters slide.
Each twist and turn, a bold new quest,
Adventures call, a fleeting jest.

The shorelines shift, the tides arrange,
Life's journey moves, it feels so strange.
With every wave and whispering tide,
A story forged where dreams abide.

Beneath the moon, reflections gleam,
A dance of light—a waking dream.
The echoes of the water flow,
In depths of hearts, we come to know.

Yet in this dance, we find our place,
In nature's hold, in time's embrace.
With every splash, we rise and fall,
In ever-changing currents, we heed the call.

A Symphony of Sweeping Emotions

In silence, hearts begin to play,
A symphony in shades of gray.
The whispers rise, a soft refrain,
From joy's bright notes to echoes of pain.

Each heartbeat thumps, each tear a key,
In this vast score of you and me.
With crescendos high and basses deep,
In this grand concert, secrets seep.

A melody of love and loss,
Each chord reminds us of the cost.
Through fleeting moments, we compose,
A tapestry of highs and lows.

The orchestra, a vibrant swath,
Transitions blend in human cloth.
Each note a brush, each pause a sigh,
In this grand symphony, we fly.

Together we create the sound,
In harmony, our souls are bound.
Through sweeping emotions, we ascend,
This symphony, our lives transcend.

Whispering Winds of Change

The whispering winds begin to sway,
Through rustling leaves, they make their way.
With gentle breath, they kiss the trees,
Unfolding tales on every breeze.

The clouds above, they shift and shape,
In driven storms, no room for escape.
Yet with each gust, new paths arise,
A chance to dream beneath the skies.

As seasons turn, so do our hearts,
In every end, a brand new start.
The wind it carries hopes untold,
In gusts of warmth, through gusts so bold.

A dance of change, we must embrace,
In every gust, we find our grace.
These whispering winds, they beckon near,
To shed our fears and conquer fear.

And so we follow where they lead,
Towards brighter days and planted seed.
In every breath of change, we find,
New dawns await, unconfined.

The Gentle Pull of the Moon's Embrace

In twilight's glow, the moon appears,
A beacon bright through all our fears.
Her gentle pull, a soft caress,
A guiding light in night's recess.

Beneath her watch, the world stands still,
The silver beams our hearts can fill.
In quietude, we find our peace,
In lunar love, our worries cease.

The tides respond to her sweet call,
In every ebb and flow, we crawl.
Her magic weaves throughout the night,
A constant source of pure delight.

In moments lost, we yearn to stay,
As dreams unfold in silver ballet.
With every phase, she shows her grace,
In cycles deep, we find our place.

So let the moon's soft whispers sway,
And cradle us till break of day.
For in her embrace, we feel alive,
The gentle pull helps us thrive.

Soliloquies of Rising and Falling

In the quiet dusk, I rise,
Thoughts like whispers fill the skies.
Fallen moments in the night,
Echoes of dreams take their flight.

The sun slips down, shadows play,
Each breath a choice, night or day.
Rising gently, hope anew,
Falling softly, fears accrue.

In stillness found, a heart beats strong,
Winds of change, we all belong.
Rising high on wings of trust,
Falling low in fragile dust.

The dance of life, a timeless spin,
Rising up, we learn to win.
Falling down, we meet the ground,
In each whisper, love is found.

Through every rise, a story told,
In every fall, we gather gold.
A tapestry of light and shade,
In solitude, our paths are laid.

The Fire and the Rain

A spark ignites, the flames ignite,
In the dark, they burn so bright.
Rain falls soft, a gentle balm,
In the storm, there's hidden calm.

Fire dances, shadows flicker,
Each heartbeat, pulsing quicker.
Raindrops fall, a soothing song,
Nature's two, where we belong.

Through the blaze, we feel the heat,
In the drizzle, hearts still meet.
Fire's passion, rain's sweet sigh,
Together they paint the sky.

In the balance, life unfolds,
Two extremes, a tale retold.
Fire gives strength, rain renews,
In every drop, a spark imbues.

From flame to drop, our lives entwine,
Through joy and pain, a sacred line.
In every storm, a fire stays,
In every blaze, the rain displays.

Shorelines of Sorrow and Joy

Waves of sorrow kiss the sand,
Footprints linger, hand in hand.
Joyful tides, they rise and swell,
Whispers of stories yet to tell.

Underneath the moonlit glow,
Both joys and tears in ebbs and flow.
Shores embrace both loss and gain,
Through every heartache, life remains.

Seagulls call, a haunting sound,
Echoes of the lost are found.
Sunshine breaks through clouds of gray,
Delighting hearts along the way.

In the silence, healing starts,
Each drop of rain restores our hearts.
Sorrow shapes the joyous sea,
In every wave, we find the key.

From grief to grace, we sail along,
In every tide, we sing our song.
Across the shores, both bright and bleak,
Sorrow and joy, the truth we seek.

Whispered Secrets of the Heart's Voyage

On a journey deep within,
Heartbeats echo, dreams begin.
Whispers secrets soft and low,
Map the paths where feelings flow.

Sailing through the winds of change,
Emotions shared, yet so estranged.
Each truth a wave, each doubt a storm,
In gentle tides, our hearts form.

In the silence, the heart reveals,
Hidden hopes, and soft appeals.
Journeys made on whispered breath,
In every choice, we dance with death.

No compass guides this fragile quest,
For in the struggle, we are blessed.
Navigating shadows, light appears,
Carried by the weight of fears.

Through every mile, we grow and bend,
Heart's voyage whispers without end.
In each secret held so tight,
We find our way through dark to light.

Flickers of Joy Amidst Dusk

As the sun kisses the night,
Whispers of laughter take flight.
Stars blink like dreams on the rise,
In shadows, hope softly lies.

Fireflies dance through the air,
Moments of bliss, rich and rare.
Holding tight to the fleeting glow,
Through dark paths, we learn to grow.

The sky wears a lavender hue,
Painting the world fresh and new.
Every sigh turns into a song,
In twilight's embrace, we belong.

As echoes paint the silhouettes,
Each heartbeat slowly begets.
In silence, we find our way home,
Through the whispers of dusk, we roam.

Underneath the vast starlit sky,
We gather dreams, and together fly.
In the dusk, joy flickers bright,
Guiding us through the gentle night.

Mosaic of Melancholy and Bliss

In corners of sorrow, we find,
Fragments of joy intertwined.
Colors that bleed, shadows that play,
A canvas where dreams drift away.

Through laughter's veil, we feel the ache,
Memories linger, the heart will quake.
Yet in this dance of dark and light,
We grasp the moments, hold them tight.

Clouds weep softly, tears that fall,
Serenity cradled in a call.
Each note of sadness, sweet and clear,
A symphony only we can hear.

Petals scatter on a breeze,
Whispers of life among the trees.
In every loss, there's a gain,
A mosaic built from joy and pain.

As the sun sets its fiery glow,
We weave our stories, high and low.
Finding peace in the tangled strife,
Embracing the fullness of life.

Through the Eye of the Heart

Glimmers of truth in the haze,
Reflections of love in a gaze.
With every heartbeat, feel the spark,
Navigating through shadows dark.

The heart's whisper, soft yet clear,
Guides us onward, year by year.
In every glance, a tale unfolds,
Hidden stories, forever told.

Through storms that challenge our will,
In quiet moments, our souls fill.
Each pulse a reminder of grace,
A delicate dance, we embrace.

In the depths of night, we see,
The light that shines within the free.
Through the eye of the heart, we find,
Peace in the chaos, love entwined.

Every tear tells a story true,
Layers of life, old and new.
Through pain and joy, we discern,
The lessons within us, we learn.

Navigating Tides of Yesterday

Waves crash softly, memories stir,
Whispers of time in gentle blur.
Sailing through echoes of the past,
Learning from tides that ebb and last.

Each moment carved in grains of sand,
Lessons linger, hand in hand.
Carrying burdens, we make our way,
Navigating dawns of yesterday.

The compass tilts with dreams once bright,
Shadows linger, yet look for light.
In the solitude of the sea,
We discover the hearts that breathe.

Reflections shimmer, stories told,
A tapestry woven, bold.
Through every high and every low,
We're sculpted by the winds that blow.

From the shores of what came before,
We step forward, evermore.
In the embrace of shifting tides,
The heart learns where hope resides.

Currents Beneath the Surface

Whispers of water move below,
Secrets that the tides can't show.
Life pulses where shadows glide,
Currents weave, the world's great tide.

Mysteries in depths untold,
Stories of the brave and bold.
In silence, treasures softly dwell,
Beneath the waves, all is well.

Ripples speak in softest tones,
Echoes of forgotten zones.
Dancers in a fluid space,
Flowing free in nature's grace.

All the while, we stand above,
Unaware of what they love.
Beneath the calm, a world awaits,
In shadowed depths, the heart pulsates.

The Canvas of Calm and Chaos

A brush of light, a stroke of dark,
In every twist, there's hope's bright spark.
Chaos revels, calm holds tight,
Together, they create the night.

Colors swirl in wild embrace,
Softness hidden in the race.
Each moment striking like a stroke,
A tale of life in colors woke.

Silent whispers meet the roar,
Life's dynamics evermore.
Chaos dances, calm observes,
In this art, the heart preserves.

With every hue, a story's spun,
Under the watching, fickle sun.
The canvas breathes, the tension grows,
In layers deep, our truth still flows.

Unraveling in Gentle Storms

A soft breeze stirs the fading light,
Whispers weave into the night.
Rain drops like gems, a sweet refrain,
Unraveling hearts in soft, warm rain.

Tears of joy and sorrow blend,
In every gust, the heart will mend.
Gentle storms hum lullabies,
Drawing forth the buried sighs.

Silhouettes in shadows sway,
Guided by the winds' soft play.
Every stumble tells a tale,
Of lasting love that will not fail.

Clouds will drift and skies will part,
Yet storms often spark the heart.
In the quiet after the fray,
Resilience blooms in light's warm ray.

Sailing Through the Shifting Sands

Sails unfurled to greet the breeze,
Oceans whisper secrets with ease.
Navigating paths unknown,
On shifting sands, we've often flown.

Waves crash upon the golden shore,
Time's embrace, forever more.
With every swell, the journey calls,
The turning tide, as daylight falls.

Sandcastles built with dreams and care,
Fleeting moments lost in air.
Yet each grain, a story told,
Of dreams pursued and hearts so bold.

The stars above begin to gleam,
Guiding us through every dream.
With courage strong, we ride the waves,
In shifting sands, the spirit saves.

Chasing the Dusk and Dawn

In the shimmer of fading light,
Shadows dance, taking flight.
Colors blend, a painter's dream,
Whispers echo, silently scream.

The horizon bows, kissing the night,
Stars awaken, hearts take flight.
Chasing moments in twilight's embrace,
Time stands still in this sacred space.

Fleeting glances of day's last glow,
Embers of warmth in the soft wind blow.
Each step a prayer, a calling loud,
In the chase of dusk, under the shroud.

Morning breaks with tender grace,
Sunrise paints the world's face.
From darkness rises a gentle song,
In the chase of dawn, we all belong.

Endless cycles of night and day,
A dance of light, leading the way.
In the chase of dusk and dawn, we find,
The beauty held in the heart and mind.

Echoes of Unspoken Words

In the silence, thoughts reside,
Words unspoken, paths denied.
Echoes linger, haunting the air,
Stories buried, hidden with care.

Eyes that shimmer, secrets concealed,
A longing heart, untruly revealed.
Moments drift like leaves in the breeze,
Between the lines, the heart takes ease.

What could have been, whispers in night,
Thoughts that linger, hiding from sight.
Chasing shadows of what we feel,
In the quiet, the heart's ideal.

Words like rivers, flow and bend,
Silent currents that never end.
Yearning to speak, yet feeling shy,
In this space, the truth can fly.

Echoes dance on the edge of dreams,
Carrying hope in silent streams.
To break the silence, to let it be heard,
Is to set free those unspoken words.

Navigating the Depths Within

In the stillness, shadows play,
Navigating through the fray.
Emotions swirl like ocean tide,
In the depths, we often hide.

Waves of doubt crash against the shore,
Seeking peace and wanting more.
Each breath a step, a journey new,
Inward paths to see what's true.

Treasures buried beneath the pain,
Glistening softly, hiding in rain.
Through stormy seas, we brave the fight,
As stars above guide our light.

With every row, the waters clear,
Facing fears, no longer sheer.
Navigating toward a brighter day,
In the depths, we learn to sway.

When silence speaks, we listen close,
To the heart's rhythm, we need the most.
In navigating the depths we find,
The beauty woven in the mind.

Flux and Fathom

In a world that shifts and sways,
Moments drift, like fleeting days.
Time ebbs and flows, a constant stream,
In flux we dance, beneath a dream.

Fathoms deep, the heart does yearn,
Lessons learned with each return.
Through tides of change, we find our way,
Embracing night, inviting day.

Change, a whisper, gentle but firm,
In its current, we surely learn.
To embrace the flux, to ride the waves,
Is to be free, and truly brave.

Each breath a reminder, nothing stays,
The essence of life in myriad plays.
Fathoms call from below the surface,
In the depths lies true purpose.

So let us wander through every turn,
Finding beauty in each new discern.
In flux and fathom, we'll find our song,
A melody sweet, where we all belong.

The Resilience of Shifting Tides

Each wave that crashes, whispers low,
A tale of struggle, taught to grow.
Beneath the surface, life persists,
In every ebb, a chance to exist.

The moon pulls gently on the sea,
Guiding paths where we can't see.
With every tide, we learn to trust,
In change, we find the core of us.

Footprints washed where we once stood,
Leaves traces in the shifting wood.
Nature's cycle, fierce yet kind,
Reminds us to keep hope aligned.

In shadows cast by fleeting light,
We stand resilient, ready for flight.
For in the depth of every wave,
Lies strength to rise, the heart to brave.

So stand with me on sandy shores,
As tides rise high, our spirit soars.
Together, face the ocean's roar,
In every change, we'll seek for more.

Crescendos of the Soul's Symphony

In quiet notes, the heartbeats play,
Melodies crafted through night and day.
Every whisper builds a refrain,
A symphony born from joy and pain.

The strings of longing, taut and true,
Resonate in the soul's deep hue.
Fingers dance on keys of fate,
Harmonies woven, never too late.

In crescendos, we rise and fall,
An echoing voice, the music calls.
With every chord, a story told,
Of passions fierce and dreams of gold.

When silence reigns, we find a way,
To hear the notes that softly sway.
For deep within, the echoes throng,
A symphony that makes us strong.

So play your part, embrace the sound,
In every heart, the notes abound.
Together we'll create a tune,
A masterpiece beneath the moon.

Serenity Amidst the Roiling Waves

Amidst the chaos, peace can thrive,
In stormy waters, we come alive.
Finding calm in the tempest's heart,
A tranquil mind, a sacred art.

The ocean's roar is fierce and bold,
Yet in its depths, warm stories hold.
We breathe the salt, embrace the rush,
In the wild, our spirits hush.

With every crash, we stand our ground,
In storm's embrace, true strength is found.
The tides may rise, yet here we stand,
Rooted firm, like ancient sand.

Look to the horizon, where peace awaits,
Even as the storm creates.
In the midst of waves, calm will shine,
A light of hope, forever mine.

For in the dance of ebb and flow,
We find the seeds of strength we sow.
With open hearts, we learn to sway,
Serenity carried on each spray.

The Stillness After the Storm

The tempest fades, the calm returns,
Amidst the quiet, the heart still burns.
Battered branches, skies now clear,
In stillness found, we shed our fear.

Raindrops linger on leaves of green,
Reflecting light in a gentle sheen.
The world resets, a breath so deep,
Promising peace from chaos's leap.

With grateful hearts, we gather round,
In silence profound, love is found.
The air is fresh, the spirit sings,
In the aftermath, the beauty clings.

Each memory of the storm persists,
Yet in this stillness, hope insists.
With every sigh, a new day dawns,
As shadows lift, the spirit yawns.

So let us stand in quiet trust,
For life resumes, and love is just.
In every pause, a lesson lies,
In the stillness, our souls rise.

Flux in the Sea of Dreams

In the silence where dreams reside,
The waves whisper secrets untold.
Drifting in hues of deep blue tide,
A treasure of wonders unfolds.

With each crest, new visions arise,
Painting the canvas of night.
Stars dance softly in twilight skies,
Guiding the vessels of light.

Currents twist, fate's winding thread,
Sails stretch taut against the breeze.
In this realm, where hope is spread,
The heart finds comfort in ease.

Wanderers seeking their path,
In the depths where shadows blend.
Through the storms and gentle swath,
They learn to bend, yet not to end.

Lost in the flow of a dream's embrace,
Each moment, a ripple in time.
While fears dissolve without a trace,
Awakening to the sublime.

The Charting of Emotional Waters

In the depths of a tranquil sea,
Emotions rise and fall like tides.
Navigating what's meant to be,
With each wave, the heart confides.

Sailing smooth on joy's bright crest,
Storms of sorrow hide beneath.
Finding solace in the quest,
A compass forged from belief.

The stars align in skies of gray,
Mapping the feelings we share.
Through the clouds, we find our way,
Tangled hearts weaving a prayer.

Charting course through shifting sands,
Where love's lighthouses brightly shine.
Together, we'll navigate lands,
Where hope and heart intertwine.

When the currents pull us apart,
We'll find strength in the unseen.
Faith will steer the wandering heart,
As we sail through the serene.

Untamed Seasons of the Heart

In spring's dance, the flowers bloom,
Whispers of love fill the air.
Summer's heat, a bright perfume,
Passion ignites without a care.

Autumn paints with golden hues,
Memories drift like wilting leaves.
Winter's chill brings quiet blues,
A time to reflect and grieve.

Each season a shift in our souls,
Joy and sorrow, ebb and flow.
Life's rhythm plays, heart's drumrolls,
Guiding us where love will grow.

Through thunderous storms and clear skies,
The heart's compass seeks the true.
In soft laughter, in bitter cries,
We find what it means to renew.

Untamed, wild, and ever free,
In this journey, together we roam.
Embracing the seasons we see,
With the heart as our eternal home.

Reflections in the Pool of Change

Beneath the surface, secrets gleam,
Ripples taint the stillness bright.
In the depths, we chase a dream,
Shadows dancing with the light.

Echoes of laughter intertwine,
Where past and present collide.
In the waters, our fates align,
As the currents turn the tide.

Each reflection, a moment caught,
Mirrored thoughts trace our intent.
Lessons learned, wisdom is sought,
In silence, our hearts lament.

The cycles we break and rebuild,
Leaves fall, yet new life ignites.
In this space, the void is filled,
Through the dark, we find the lights.

Change is constant, ebbing flow,
In the pool of the heart's design.
Embracing all that we may know,
In the water, our souls align.

Tides of the Heart

In the moon's gentle glow, warmth resides,
Love flows like the sea, where time abides.
Each wave brings a whisper, soft and sweet,
Tides pull and release, where lovers greet.

The shore wears our footprints, memories dear,
With every rise and fall, you feel me near.
The ocean's heartbeat echoes our embrace,
In this salty air, we find our place.

As the currents dance and play with the sand,
We sway to the rhythm, hand in hand.
The depth of your gaze, a vast, endless sea,
Together we'll sail, just you and me.

Through storms we shall wander, steadfast and true,
Navigating life's course, just I and you.
With the tide as our guide, we'll never part,
Forever bound by the tides of the heart.

So let the waves crash, let the winds blow,
In this ocean of love, we'll ever glow.
For as long as the tide rises and falls,
In the depths of our hearts, love quietly calls.

Waves of Whispered Feelings

Softly, the waves tell secrets of the night,
Every splash a story, a flickering light.
In the hush of the moon, our thoughts unfold,
Whispers carried on breezes, warmth from the cold.

Gentle caresses, like fingers on skin,
Sharing our dreams, where our hearts begin.
Each echo a promise, a vow we hold tight,
In the calm of the ocean, we take our flight.

The tide brings us closer, hearts intertwined,
Every glance a treasure, a love so kind.
With each rhythmic pulse, emotions collide,
In the depths of our souls, together we ride.

As shadows dance lightly upon the shore,
We listen to whispers, forevermore.
The waves lull our hearts, tender and free,
In the ocean's embrace, just you and me.

So here we will stay, in silence profound,
With waves of emotions, in love's soft sound.
For every whisper speaks of moments we share,
In the tides of our feelings, we're beyond compare.

The Dance of Highs and Lows

In the twilight's glow, shadows extend,
Hearts sway like the tide, with curves that bend.
Highs lift us up, the world feels so bright,
Lows bring us close, in the softest of nights.

Waves crash and recede, in rhythm they play,
We dance through the storms, come what may.
Each rise is a triumph, each fall, a lesson,
In the dance of our hearts, we find our expression.

The pull of the tide, a force we can't see,
Yet in every movement, you're here next to me.
Our laughter, like bubbles, floats up to the air,
In the waltz of our souls, a love so rare.

So let the highs lift us, let the lows bind,
In this beautiful chaos, our hearts intertwine.
With every step forward, we learn how to flow,
Together we blossom, in the dance that we know.

Through every cycle, through every refrain,
In the heart of the ocean, our love will remain.
For in the dance of life, through each ebb and rise,
We find our forever beneath endless skies.

Currents of Quiet Reflection

Silently flowing, the river of time,
Currents of thought, in rhythm and rhyme.
With each gentle ripple, we ponder and see,
The essence of life, how it shapes you and me.

Beneath the soft surface, deep truths lie,
In the calm of the waters, we question why.
Moments of stillness, our souls intertwine,
Finding reflections, the sacred divine.

Whispers of memories, like leaves on the stream,
We drift on the surface, lost in our dream.
Mapping the journey, each turn like a song,
In the current of thoughts, we both belong.

Time may flow swiftly, like clouds in the blue,
Yet anchored in stillness, I find peace in you.
In the depth of these waters, our spirits take flight,
Guided by whispers that dance in the night.

So let the river carry us, gentle and true,
In currents of quiet, where love feels anew.
For as long as we ponder, together we find,
In the depths of reflection, we leave fear behind.

The Language of Falling Leaves

Whispers of gold drift through the air,
Each leaf a story, a breath, a prayer.
Time folds softly in shades of decay,
Nature's soft sigh as it finds its way.

Crimson hues brush the paths we tread,
Memories linger where silence is spread.
A rustle of secrets, a chirp from a tree,
In the dance of the wind, we hear the plea.

Beneath the boughs where shadows lay,
The heart beats softly, it yearns to stay.
Embrace the chill, let the colors ignite,
In the language of leaves, we find our light.

A carpet of whispers on the ground,
Each step a rhythm, a pulse, a sound.
Seasons change but the stories remain,
In the whispering leaves, we find our refrain.

So let them fall, let them weave their tale,
In the autumn's breath, let us set sail.
For in each descent, life finds its grace,
In the language of leaves, we find our place.

Interludes of Radiant Surrender

In twilight's glow, hearts gently unfold,
Stories converge in whispers untold.
A moment suspended, the world slows down,
In luminous shades, dreams dance around.

Stars twinkle softly, a celestial cue,
In the quiet night, we find something true.
Soft laughter echoes, the air is alive,
In radiant surrender, our spirits thrive.

Through gentle sighs, passions ignite,
Interludes shimmer, bathing us in light.
In time's fluid embrace, we feel anew,
A tapestry woven in silver and blue.

Glistening moments, like dew on the grass,
Subtle as moonlight, our worries they pass.
Together we drift, on waves of delight,
Finding our way in the soft of the night.

So let us embrace this transient scene,
In interludes cherished, where love is seen.
As daylight falters, let surrender be,
A radiant promise, just you and me.

Shadows Dance with Light in Turn

In the twilight's veil, shadows gently sway,
With light's soft touch, they begin to play.
A ballet of whispers where the day meets night,
In this tender dance, everything feels right.

Echoes of laughter fill the open space,
Where the sun's last rays caress a face.
In every flicker, a promise is spun,
Shadows and light, forever as one.

Golden hues melt into deepening gray,
As silhouettes lengthen, weaving their play.
In the quiet embrace, a story unfolds,
Of lives intertwined, both timid and bold.

Moments caught fire in the twilight's breath,
Dance with the shadows, defying death.
In harmony's rhythm, we find our way,
With shadows as partners, in night's ballet.

So dwell in the spaces where dark meets the bright,
In shadows that linger, 'neath stars of the night.
For every dance has a story to share,
In the light and the shadow, love's true affair.

The Flow of Unfinished Stories

Winds carry whispers of tales left to tell,
Each heart a chapter, a sweet wishing well.
Moments like riverbanks shaping the flow,
In the unfinished stories, we find we grow.

Pages of life come with ink that runs free,
Plots twist and turn like the bright, restless sea.
Characters linger, just out of our sight,
In the creased corners of day turning night.

Every glance, every touch, a new line to write,
In the tapestry woven, threads shining bright.
A journey that's endless, where paths intertwine,
In the flow of our stories, your hand in mine.

The beauty of pauses, of spaces between,
In the art of the silence, in what might have been.
Each breath a new stanza, each heartbeat a rhyme,
In the unfinished stories, we capture time.

So let us embrace all that winds through the seams,
In the flow of our stories, we weave our dreams.
For though pages are missing, the book still survives,
In the flow of unfinished, our spirit revives.

Which Way the Wind Will Blow?

The trees sway gently in the breeze,
Whispers of fate on the autumn leaves.
Clouds drift slowly, painting the sky,
Wondering where the heart must fly.

Each gust carries tales untold,
Secrets of dreams, both brave and bold.
A compass lost, yet stars still gleam,
Guiding the soul toward a distant dream.

With every shift, the course may change,
Paths diverge, a life rearranged.
But in the storm, there's beauty found,
In chaos, hope's sweet sound.

So follow the breeze, let it unfold,
Trust your spirit to be brave and bold.
For in the winds that twist and twine,
You'll find your heart, forever entwined.

Navigating the Emotional Horizon

Across the waves of joy and pain,
Sailing forth, the heart's refrain.
A sunrise glimmers on the sea,
Charting paths to set us free.

Beneath the surface, currents hide,
Emotions swell like the rising tide.
Hope and fear, a constant fight,
Navigating wrong and right.

Each wave brings lessons from the past,
Moments fleeting, yet they last.
In every swell, a chance to grow,
To learn the depth of what we know.

As horizons beckon with a glow,
Together we'll find how far to go.
With every tear and every smile,
We'll sail through stormy seas awhile.

Whirlpools of Memories Past

In the stillness, echoes call,
Whirlpools swirling, memories fall.
Fragments of laughter, shadows of tears,
Caught in cycles, lost in years.

Faces fade, yet stories remain,
In every heart, a silent pain.
Moments captured in fleeting light,
Hoping to hold them, wrong or right.

As pages turn, the tale unfolds,
Whispers of love and truths retold.
In watery depths, the past does sway,
Guiding our steps in the light of day.

Diving deeper into life's embrace,
Finding solace in the human race.
For each whirlpool is a thread,
Weaving the fabric of dreams we've bred.

The Undercurrents of Human Experience

Beneath the surface lies a sea,
Waves of thought, emotions set free.
Current flows through joy and strife,
The undercurrents of our life.

In silence speaks the heart's own tune,
Dancing shadows beneath the moon.
The pulse of memories, sweet and raw,
Revealing truths that leave us in awe.

Clashing tides with every choice,
A symphony, yet so much noise.
In the struggle, we find our strength,
Navigating the depths, at length.

In every wave, we learn to trust,
To rise from ashes, to turn to dust.
Embrace the journey, its twists and bends,
For within the chaos, life transcends.

Voices in the Undercurrent

Whispers dance beneath the waves,
Secrets lost, in silence staves.
Echoes of the heart's refrain,
Yearning calls, a sweet disdain.

Ripples weave through shadowed dreams,
Softly flowing, where light gleams.
Voices rise, though none can see,
Their tales told in mystery.

In the depths, where few will tread,
Silent stories linger, spread.
Bound to currents, swift and free,
They sing of what it means to be.

Underneath, the world persists,
Vibrant hues in misty trysts.
Each note lingers like a prayer,
Carried far beyond despair.

In the dark, together blend,
Voices of the lost transcend.
An eternal song set loose,
In the deeps, a haunting muse.

The Weight of a Feather's Fall

Softly drifting through the air,
Gentle touch without a care.
Silent in its tender flight,
The feather whispers to the night.

Graceful arcs, a soft goodbye,
A moment's peace before the sigh.
Fragile dreams upon the breeze,
Secrets held among the trees.

The weight it carries, light yet deep,
Memories that the heart must keep.
Abandoned hopes, yet newly found,
In the quiet, love surrounds.

Each descent, a dance of fate,
On the brink, we contemplate.
How such lightness can unfold,
In the stories yet untold.

For in falling, life reveals,
The beauty woven in what heals.
With every drift, a tale recalls,
The weight of a feather's fall.

Dunes of Despair

Endless sands stretch far and wide,
Beneath the sun, hopes often hide.
Waves of sorrow, shifting ground,
In each grain, lost dreams are found.

Whispers tumble in the breeze,
Gritty echoes, searching pleas.
Crimson skies reflect the pain,
Stories buried, washed in rain.

Through the valleys, shadows creep,
Memories of what we keep.
A weary heart, a barren land,
Loneliness, like shifting sand.

But in the dusk, a spark remains,
Shining bright through dark refrains.
Hope flickers, ignites the night,
Against despair, it holds its light.

So tread the dunes, though hard and cruel,
Each step brings strength, a different rule.
For in the emptiness, we find,
The beauty of the heart unlined.

Peaks of Hope

Higher still, the mountains rise,
Touching softly painted skies.
Each summit holds a promise clear,
Whispers of what we hold dear.

Scaling cliffs with steady breath,
Defying shadows, conquering death.
Through the storms, we seek the light,
Finding strength in every fight.

Beneath the stars, dreams take flight,
Guided by the moon's pure light.
The path ahead, while steep and steep,
Offers solace that we keep.

In the silence, courage grows,
While time's river slowly flows.
Hope's embrace, a tender bind,
Uniting souls, hearts intertwined.

Each peak we climb, a story told,
Resilience wrapped in bands of gold.
Together we shall rise and soar,
On peaks of hope, forevermore.

Shimmering Moments of Stillness

In the hush of twilight's call,
Time suspends, and shadows fall.
A gentle sigh, a subtle pause,
Embracing peace without a cause.

Ripples dance on silver streams,
Where reality meets our dreams.
Each second glows, a spark of grace,
In every whisper, we find our place.

Light cascades through leaves of green,
Moments captured, soft and serene.
The world slows down, we breathe in deep,
Finding joy in quiet we keep.

Candles flicker, shadows play,
As day surrenders to the gray.
In stillness, hearts and minds align,
Forever held in love's design.

So take a breath, let worries part,
In shimmering stillness, find your heart.
For in these moments, life reveals,
The beauty that true stillness feels.

The Rhythm of Broken Halos

In twilight's gleam, where shadows play,
The whispers of lost dreams drift away.
With every chord, a silent plea,
As hope takes flight, it longs to be.

Fractured light through ancient trees,
Echoes swirl on the evening breeze.
Breaking moments, sighs descend,
In quiet dusk, beginnings blend.

Yet in the cracks, new seeds arise,
From shattered paths, the spirit flies.
Each halo worn but still aglow,
In brokenness, we find our flow.

Through autumn leaves, the memories drift,
A gentle touch, the heart's soft gift.
We dance in shadows, bright and bold,
The tale of life in whispers told.

As night enfolds, the stars awake,
In every sigh, the world will shake.
With rhythm found in every fall,
We rise once more, we heed the call.

Glistening Raindrops of Release

Beneath the clouds, the world takes breath,
Each droplet falls, a dance with death.
In every splash, a story speaks,
Of whispered dreams and future peaks.

The silver beads on leaves do cling,
A symphony of nature's spring.
With every drop, the earth awakes,
A melody of life it makes.

In fleeting moments, sorrows drown,
As rain cascades, we shed the crown.
The weight of years, now washed away,
In glistening light, we find our way.

Through puddles deep, reflections form,
A canvas bright beneath the storm.
Each ripple tells of love and loss,
In every wave, we pay the cost.

At last, we breathe in freshened air,
With every raindrop, burdens share.
The heart finds light, the soul released,
In rain's embrace, we are at peace.

Turning Pages of Silent Storms

In chapters dark, our whispers fade,
The ink of storms a silent trade.
With every shift, new tales unfold,
In time-worn books, our truths are told.

The shadows stretch like aged hands,
Through tempest winds, the heart withstands.
Each turning leaf, a silent prayer,
In storm's embrace, we learn to dare.

Echoes of thunder, a distant call,
As moments linger, we rise or fall.
With courage found in written lines,
We brave the waves, our fate aligns.

In stillness found, we pause and see,
The power in a memory.
As pages turn, new dreams ignite,
Through silent storms, we find our light.

Beyond the tempest, calm will break,
With every heart, a journey make.
In tales of woe, we find the grace,
Through turning pages, we find our place.

The Echo of Heartbeats and Currents

In twilight's hush, the whispers flow,
The gentle pulse of river's glow.
With every beat, the echoes call,
In water's stride, we learn to fall.

The dance of time in soft embrace,
With heartbeats synced, we find our pace.
A current strong, it weaves and winds,
In every pulse, a truth unwinds.

As night descends, the stars align,
In silent rhythm, souls entwine.
Through ebbs and flows, we chase the night,
In every shadow, we find the light.

With every spark, a story starts,
The echo resonates in hearts.
In currents deep, we trust the flow,
As love ignites, we learn to grow.

In every wave, a memory lies,
The dance of life beneath vast skies.
In heartbeats shared, our spirits soar,
Through every echo, we seek more.

The Cascade of Changing Moods

A gentle breeze whispers low,
Colors shift as feelings grow.
Sunshine fades to shadowed hue,
Emotions dance, the skies turn blue.

Laughter echoes in the air,
Clouds of doubt begin to stare.
Raindrops fall with thunder's song,
In this chaos, we belong.

Joy spills over like a stream,
Hope ignites the fading dream.
In the swirl of night and day,
Hearts can mend, or drift away.

Twilight glimmers, thoughts unwind,
Anchors lost but peace will find.
As the stars begin to shine,
Moods will shift, and all align.

Through the tempest and the calm,
Nature's pulse a healing balm.
In each moment, breathe it in,
The cascade flows, let change begin.

Inhale the Stillness, Exhale the Waves

Inhale the calm, let it fill,
With every breath, find your will.
Here in silence, thoughts subside,
In this moment, you can hide.

Exhale the doubts, release the fear,
Let the waves of peace draw near.
Feel the rhythm, rise and fall,
Each soft whisper, nature's call.

Between the breaths, a space so wide,
A tranquil heart, a gentle guide.
Drifting softly on the sea,
Let the currents set you free.

Nestled deep in the embrace,
Find your pulse, your sacred space.
Time stands still, and here you stay,
Inhale the stillness, drift away.

Waves of thoughts, they come and go,
Among the tides, you come to know.
Every moment, perfect grace,
With each breath, find your place.

Journey Through the Emotional Tide

Waves of feeling start to rise,
In this journey, truth belies.
From the depths, we seek to find,
Connections woven, heart entwined.

Beneath the surface, shadows sway,
Rising currents pull away.
In the ebb and flow, we grow,
With every tide, our joys bestow.

Shores of sorrow, peaks of glee,
In this odyssey, we see.
Mapping out the highs and lows,
Crafting joy from tears that flow.

Through the storms, we learn to sail,
Anchored firm when we unveil.
Journey forth, embrace the ride,
Through the emotional tide.

Every wave, a lesson learned,
With each crest, our passion burned.
Navigating every phase,
In the tide's embrace, we blaze.

The Cradle of Calm and Chaos

In the cradle, peace will nest,
Where chaos dances, hearts can rest.
Gentle whispers soothe the storm,
Through the noise, find your form.

Between the clamor, silence waits,
Holding tight to love, not fates.
Swings of balance, life portrayed,
In the quiet, fears can fade.

Walk the line of dark and light,
In this cradle, dreams take flight.
Strengthened by the ebb and flow,
Chaos teaches what we know.

With every pause, there comes a chance,
In confusion's whirl, we still can dance.
Calm within the raging storm,
In the cradle, hearts reform.

Embrace the restless, hold it dear,
In every heartbeat, calm is near.
At the intersection, truth resides,
In the cradle of life's wild rides.